# Running Out of Words for Afterwards

# Running Out of Words for Afterwards

Poems by
## David Hargreaves

Broadstone

Copyright © 2021 by David Hargreaves

Library of Congress Control Number 2021944643

ISBN 978-1-937968-93-9

Cover artwork "Running Out of Words"
by Natalie E. Laswell,
used by permission.

Broadstone Books
An Imprint of
Broadstone Media LLC
418 Ann Street
Frankfort, KY 40601-1929
BroadstoneBooks.com

*for N.E.L.*

## Contents

ONE

    No Tongue Can Tell / 3
    What I Wanted / 4
    Now & Then / 5
    No One's Land / 6
    Rule of Threes / 7
    Saṃsāra / 10
    Gray Matter / 12
    News at Eleven / 13
    Estimated Time of Arrival / 14
    River / 15

TWO

    Lunch with Gautam / 19
    Biopsy / 20
    Prosthetic / 21
    Vacancies / 22
    Recognition / 26
    God of the Gaps / 27
    Prāṇ / 28
    Umbra / 29
    The Library Window / 30
    Backwards Through the Dark / 32

THREE

    Dream Vista / 35
    Gull Woman / 36
    If Only / 37
    Call Before You Dig / 38
    Earthshine / 39
    Awe is Real / 40

## FOUR

Elegy for an Election / 47
Learning Curve / 48
See and Be Seen / 49
Restless Leg Syndrome / 50
Ode to the Fern / 52
Ins and Outs / 53
Boon / 56
Continental Divide / 58
Step in the Same River Twice / 60

## FIVE

Afterimage / 63
Mayfly Diary / 64
Mayfly Diary / 65
Mayfly Diary / 66
Mayfly Diary / 67
Mayfly Diary / 68
Mayfly Diary / 69
Nature/Nurture / 70

## SIX

For Araniko / 73
Sense and Reference / 74
Ordinary Language / 75
Gṛdhrakūṭa / 76
Recursion / 77
Language Lesson / 78

NOTES / 80

Acknowledgments / 83

About the Author / 85

# I entreat myself

*I am, it's true, a setting sun.*
*Yes, I can set, but so what? I'll rise*
*and it's like I'm already done,*
*all along it never feels real.*

*So eyes, you be me and truly see,*
*and heart, you be the real me and weep.*
*And even if it's only at the last moment,*
*I've bet my life on this ending.*

Durga Lal Shrestha

# One

## No Tongue Can Tell
*Teku, Kathmandu*

Crossing the Bagmati River at night,
we could see from the Black Bridge
fires along the riverbank, smell

cremation, a language
of flame without words
for tongue or lick,

yet in translation
we'd drink smoke
from cigarettes as if straws

and moonshine
high-poured into shallow clay cups,
frothy bubble-eyes winking.

Each dawn
pigeons on my window ledge
mumbled love

while an old man
opened a different window,
ratcheted up his morning phlegm,

gobbed into the courtyard
three floors down,
scattering chickens.

Do you wonder as I do
is all this connected?

Taxi horns and the peal of a temple bell.

Do you wonder
is anything not?

## What I Wanted

I used to dream of being ravished,
decomposed into smutty loam,
then reborn a luscious fern
or redwood trunk thrusting

skyward above the arms
of maple saplings praying
to what little light chaos allotted.
What I got instead—

a quota of koi and lily-pads floating
on duckweed-sedated ponds,
appetite tame as house plants
hung from macramé parachutes

dropped onto sweater-vest lawns
with groin-high hedges. All I do now
is sit and sip wine beside the new
fountain while the old fountain

pens sign the treaty, the latest Versailles,
concession to the bonsai garden
path, so Zen clean shaven, so well pruned,
yet always, always thirsty.

## Now & Then
*kālī—feminine form of 'to enumerate...time...events...fate'*
    Monier-Williams, Sanskrit-English Dictionary,


O' Kālī, O' Time the Destroyer, when
was the last time you got carded?
It's all so different now

from back in the day when no one dared
utter your name, back when no one believed
in numbers, back when I first saw you

standing among the goatherds,
drink-horn in hand, straw-picking teeth,
elbow propped on the fence. You taught us

to tally the herd at dawn,
to set aside one bone-carved chit
for each goat driven out the gate

and when at dusk the goats returned,
to match goat to chit, then reckon
the difference, day from night.

Each one passes paired with a token.
Each one's branded with a burning font.
Everyone cries for their lives

whenever you say—*Time!*
O' Kālī, each day I rub the chit
in my pocket, and count myself

lucky to be seen at all
down the line of your index finger
pointed like a pistol.

## No One's Land

Main Street line of parking meters, canvas hoods,
hostage style, cinched over their heads.
*No Parking.* A parade is coming soon.

Across the street, in Memory Park,
like quail fleeing an active shooter
or marchers pummeled by water cannon,

leaves scatter across the lawn. A red cap
holds the leaf blower. Seagulls, at least,
know how to chill totemic on light poles

waiting for trickle down *fries with that?*
Turns out I've misread the shadows,
lost track of noon, missed my bus, so I text

my friend *meet at The Doomed*—a bookstore,
arteries clogged with paperbacks stacked waist high
in the aisle. I browse for a while. On the counter

The Book of Poetry lies open, first poem
scansion penciled above each syllable, a few words
glossed in Chinese with a fine-tipped pen.

My friend strolls through the door, their hair
vintage Rossetti red, paired nicely with plum lips.
They skim the poem, cross out one character,

write in the correct one, then turn and ask me
if I want to pet their velvet maroon dress
before they pivot back to the poem, dismissively—

*Humph! No one prefers the pronoun 'it.'*

## Rule of Threes

—*a dream receding* leaves behind

a tideline wrack of stranded

driftwood, shell and pebble

surf-rolled, randomized,

let go, a shoreline swath

of stochastic beauty,

beach detritus arrayed

in bell curves plotting

the chance of a lifetime,

the chance of my brother

drowning, my wife's cancer.

—*a dream of more* pebbles

raked in their bed

by the braided waters

of a stream where salmon

spawn out, rot in shallows,

where collared doves coo

Unitarian hymns

above quiet pools,

where lazy eddies

swirl and shades

drift between trees.

*—a dream of black* hoods

on sapphire jays

flocking in the tops of fir trees,

my tutelary deities

scolding. They all know me

as I am

carried along by the current,

inner tube leaking

like an old dictionary

running out of words

for afterwards.

## Saṃsāra

*'wandering...succession... rebirth...*
*mundane existence...worldly illusion'*
          Monier-Williams, Sanskrit-English Dictionary

*I saw a man pursing the horizon.*
       Stephen Crane


Eternal as a Netflix series,
end and beginning, another season.
Here's the recap: shaken awake
to monsoon lightning
in a thunder-tossed bed, an earthquake,
rattling tiles on the temple roof,

rain-flooded streets conceal
a dangerous crack in the cobblestone.
Another inkling of me ago—a girl,
maroon school-uniformed riding her bike
past the temple, tire striking the hidden gap,
untruing spokes, misshaping the wheel.

Clouds gather my wits, the sun,
a memory on my face,
a jet-haired woman in a red sari
comes with a tray
of yoghurt, flowers, vermillion powder,
kneels at my stone-sculptured feet to place
an offering—for me

the boy whose head
lopped off by his jealous father, Lord Siva,
got reborn as an elephant.
Another case of identity
theft, another way of being misled.

And always this craving, this thirst
for release, to let go the world
seen through green eyes—me,
taut smile, haybale blond,
meth-wrung carny at the county fair,
leveraging the Tilt-a-Whirl.

My skin itches wearing this saffron robe.

## Gray Matter

*Adult males are grayish above*
*with a dark trailing edge on the wings.*
                Cornell Lab of Ornithology


I'm attracted to wetlands not just for the beauty
of Linnaeus and Darwin's legalese,
but for the miles of ponderous mire,
cattail flowers in various stages
of fray, like my brain waves
of wispy cotton drifting among
the chatter of redwing blackbirds, past
oases of memory: duckweed, pond-lily
(*lemonoidae, nuphar*) since you asked.

I'm drawn to wetlands not just for the gist
between the lines of sedge and reed
thickets, bittern's galumph or wren's
territorial prattle, but for the sacred
weekend in May when grosbeak's lollygag
trill glissandos through Mother's Day
preaching from an ash grove, truth
universal as pollen, reminding me
*call mom, she knew* the Latin names
for all the birds, but now she's forgotten
even mine. Still the words

in the Gospel of Peterson tell me
northern harrier (*Circus hudsonius*),
my avatar hunting low over the marsh,
still carries within an insatiable want,
third eye scanning my inner life
for the slightest sign of voles.

## News at Eleven

I wait for the telephone call in darkness
while the latest news drizzles down Cedar Creek.
My head begins ringing. It's mother, of course.

She's likely relapsed, once more detached from all
the everyday meanings of words. I notice
she has mistaken herself for the weather

again. She tells me *the dog circled his bed
three times before lying down to sleep, surely
a sign it'll get worse*, abruptly hangs up.

I picture her now sinking deep in the couch,
Dad's barometer wrapped in her arms. I'm sure
she's back now working the creek bed, eroding

herself a new niche between boulders of grief
while low-hung cedar fronds dip in the water,
palsy with the current in time with the news.

## Estimated Time of Arrival
*8:37 p.m., January 14th, 2020*

*Well, we knocked the bastard off!*
        Edmund Hillary on summiting Everest

*We have climbed the mountain,*
*There's nothing more to do.*
        Donald Justice

*This is the Christ who climbs the sky better than airmen*
*He holds the world record for altitude.*
        Guillaume Apollinaire


The Nepal Bhasa word for 'chit-chat,' 'gossip,' 'shoot the breeze' is *gaph*,
rhymes with 'cough,' instead of 'gaff'—how to know
when English letters are asymptomatic?...*this is your captain speaking*

I close my glossary, drop my phone on accident
into the gap between the seats, folks crowding the aisle
for window pics of nothing...*out the right-hand side of the aircraft*

but haze and smog where Everest is—supposedly.
What makes a mountain a celebrity?...*our descent into Kathmandu*

Is it altitude? The dream of ascension, head in the clouds,
a sickness, a lack
of oxygen swelling the brain...*please wait for the seat-belt sign to be turned off*

Or elevation? Measured in feet on the ground, down-to-earth
thousand-dollar climbing boots and selfies
on the summit...*contents may have shifted during the flight*

On the edge of the valley, a hillside path traverses
terraced green paddy. Monsoon clouds obscure
snowcapped revelations, unleash a torrent
down a boulder-strewn ravine
to someday level with the sea....*welcome to Tribhuvan International Airport.*

# River
by Cittadhar Hṛdaya


On the road, whenever I rose
there was no one.
Along the way, wanting friends,
no one joined me.

Traveling alone in foreign circles,
I had to fit in,
gain entry, garnering little by little
respect in their eyes.

Lakes couldn't corner me
nor mountains block me.
My self-assurance frightened them.
Unable to bully me, they gave up.

Still, some witless so-called men
pressured me
as if my insights
were simply found under rocks, or in trees.

Nowadays worn by life's sorrows,
I'm unable to be worldly.
Unable to understand me,
they all say I'm escapist.

Reaching now my beloved ocean—
Behold! There!
The fire beneath the sea remains
tranquil and patient.

As I reach the end, he smiles
comforting me with love.
It's time I go, why keep him waiting?
So what if they call me coward!

# Two

## Lunch with Gautam
*If you meet a Buddha, kill the Buddha.*
         attributed to Zen Master Linji


I tell him I suffer from desire. I know
about hungry ghosts, mouths too small
to ever satisfy their cavernous appetites.

But why, I ask, would they turn up autumn
afternoon, after the Horse Creek fire smoke
finally cleared to cloudless blue? And why here?

Hovering in their black-yellow jackets, teardrop
bodies tapered down to a stinger, menacing
inches above our corncob butter-soaked paper plates

rife with peach-pie syrup and salmon
bones. They have no desire, I point out,
for Pino Gris or mindful sativa to feed

their heads. One lands on my fork tine,
another follows its nose, drawn to what's
beneath Tara's skirt. I don't understand

all the different schools of Buddhism.
Can these hungry ghosts smell cancer
as well as fear? Is getting stung karma?

First frost, he tells me
they all die off. Is it wrong,
I ask, I want to kill them anyway?

## Biopsy

The plump hunchback raccoon shrugs,
then turns away, unabashed. My flashlight

scalpels clear margins around her
summer dark by the garbage bins.

She looks back, beam-lit teeth, hisses,
then turns again, as she and her young

spiral the fir trunk
to the first limb over the patio.

I hate that sound—claws
clicking across the awning.

## Prosthetic

Overhead, night geese search
the frozen surface
> *In lotus pose, sits gray marble Buddha*
> *left hand in his lap, palm up,*

below. A woman struggles
to remind herself
> *right hand reaching downward, fingers*
> *chipped off by vandals, trying*

to be mindful; it could be so
much worse.
> *to touch the earth, call it*
> *to witness*

Practice detachment
she struggles
> *in a winter garden overgrown with ivy.*
> *Overhead, geese continue to seek*

to remind herself. Unhooking
her bra, she places
> *while he can never reach*
> *the ground.*

the new breast
on the nightstand.

## Vacancies

I.     Dusk

when the B-side

of cottonwood leaves

supplicate

to the diminished

light

and are told—*don't cry*

*or I'll give you something*

*to cry about.*

II.     Memory

the inherited family

disease of attic

scrapbook

pages of nothing

but empty

corner-holders, glued

with Elmer's

framing everything

as loss.

III.     Beaten path

of the blue-bottle fly

panic-attacked

in my black and white

tile bathroom—

tracing, re-tracing

a figure-eight

his own personal

infinity-shaped

lack of imagination.

IV.     Unreflective

and unreflected

in the neon

green slime-coated pond

winged ephemera parley

with the afterlife

while fork-tailed swallows

bank and roll underwriting

in cursive paths

a poetics of hunger.

## Recognition

Beneath a span of faded green girders,
the snowmelt-swollen river
reinvents history along its banks.

Mud-clumped leaves stranded
in willow and dogwood shrubs speak
of higher water. No more

homeless tarps or sleeping bags, only
an overturned grocery cart.
An ambulance races across the bridge

while Easter gales rip cedar shake
off the roof of the Baptist church.
Wild gusts drive geese to huddle

in corn stubble, heads bowed.
Coyote stalks a nearby field, sniffing
under clods. I get a call from dad.

*It's your brother; you need to come home.*
Beside the airport parking lot,
a kestrel hovers over unmown grass.

Frogs chorus in nearby ditches
reminding me in ancient Greece they sang
heroes into the underworld. Forgetting

where I parked my car,
I sweep the rows, fob in hand,
looking for a sign.

## God of the Gaps
*Find God in what we know, not in what we don't know.*
          Dietrich Bonhoeffer

*for my brother*


To explain what is not—god
of the gaps—enigmatic cracks
in the sidewalk, stubbing
my sandal-bare toes on.

To fear—god
of Job's fabled tête-à-tête
with desert whirlwind
sound effects from sandpaper
rubbed on cedar blocks,
ersatz radio theatre.

To feel deeply
the presence—god
of being
Arjun's charioteer, dharma
taking the reins—blue god
Krishna, lover to wide-eyed
cowherd maidens.

To resist—goddess
of spite and the Herculean
torments, yet adore
she who watches over
brave homunculus
lashed to the mast, wax
in everyone else's ears.

To be the subject of—god
the predicate of dark water,
god of lungs, god of everyone's
first truth and last breath.

## PRĀṆ

*'breath...wind...life-force...spirit'*
            Monier-Williams, Sanskrit-English Dictionary


Asleep on the couch, I'm startled
by the Lawn-Mower yanked to life

on the first pull, outside the open window,
my heart rancored by its two-cycle insult

to my inner life, with its gunshot
report each time the blade strikes

an exposed root or hurls a pebble.
Oily exhaust rankles my nose

into a memory of its opposite,
the scent of temple incense. I recall

awakening once
as if through an open window

hearing the Leaf-Blower whisper
among Godavari's trees,

a spirit gently moving the leaves.
I could feel it

across my cheeks,
*prāṇ*—'breath, breeze.'

# Umbra

*Sometimes even the sun puts on*
*a grin to beg for time off.*
              Durga Lal Shrestha


Suddenly, everyone's staring at me
from behind black shades
midway along my path

of totality. Disquieted
crows flock in the oak grove
bewildered
by noontime's crescent shadows.

I was worshipped once
as a god, but now I hate
my day job, tasked

to globalize—warm
this prairie,

heat that forest,

crack these mudflats,

parch that stream—
what's left is stagnant

water surface-tensioned
with aimless white
cottonwood seed,

a shrinking shallow pool
hunched over
by the black-crowned night
heron on a log hunting crawdads.

## The Library Window
*Nonsense is normal in The Library.*
        Borges

We all were fretting
will the drought break
before the ferns on the boulevard
turn brittle brown,
and then like lepers
lose their fingers.

So it made sense
when clouds coaxed in
from the ocean let down,
we didn't mind the parking lot drizzle,
the rainbow oil-slicks surrounding
the coffee kiosk

painted pumpkin and lime,
so long as cars still
idled in line for lattes
and Americanos. But our elders,
who knew their weather,
furrowed their brows,

noting how dusty Main Street seemed,
no longer clogged with farm machinery,
no muscular tractors,
no pesticide sprayers
with long-armed nozzles
folded like wings,

no more hay-rigs holding up traffic,
annoying the hybrids and SUVs
already late for couples counseling.
Yet, not until the bohemian waxwings
gathered like poets
in ash trees thirsting

to gorge on the last orange berries,
get garrulous drunk, and fly
smack dab into the library window,
did we admit the heat was news
that's staying news.

## Backwards Through the Dark

*Here is the absurd*
*Grinning like an idiot,*
*and the omnivorous quotidian*
*Which will have its day*
        Conrad Aiken


Midnight curls up cold unloved
as moss on a putting green. Owlets
preen in a tree in the rough. When it comes
moonlight brings momma with mice. Evening

walks up, bowlegged debutante, rickets
in spike high heels, orders twilight-
flavored vodkas. They make love
in a love seat to settle the bet. Dusk
consolidates credit card debt. Afternoon

works the swing shift, a lonely Jack Russell
on a pogo-stick watching his boy walk up
the drive, home from school. It wants to
retire at sixty-five but can't. Midday

arrives, foiling its own shadow attempt
to explode. Return it if you have the receipt.
It can't compete in the marketplace. Noon
is made cheaper overseas. Did you know dawn

bruised so easily? Blood thinners
coursing, blue and yellow
sunrise on rusty hinges, morning
shuffling in with a walker.

# Three

## Dream Vista

The Pacific swells and rolls unhurried,
sidling up to a jagged cliff
along the coastline, then exhales—
*harmonic wave oscillation*
oceanographers love to say. Yet were the sea

still a god, we'd say it *slumbers*.
Ebb and flow, each high followed
by a low trough exposing *Mollusca*-
crusted fissures, cracks recessed
deep into crevices teeming

with shifty-eyed marine lowlife,
clammed-up, clinging to rocks—the usual
riff-raff of the unconscious.

## Gull Woman

*When you sailed away*
*My goodbyes were the gulls in your wake.*
          Nuala Ní Dhomhnail


They say Gull Woman
used to mix men
Sazeracs, rye with bitters,
and serve them peanuts.

She may even have once
or twice swallowed
some sad husband's last call,
but that's all over since
that night, her eyes tear-smeared
in the bar mirror caught
a glimpse of her own divinity
and cracked
the code programming her
to serve those greedy
sea birds crying for crumbs.

Nowadays, while the dawn mist burns
and distantly a Giacometti
in waders casts into the surf,
the gulls flock the opposite way,
tracking the shoreline
through the haze
to throng above her, hovering
on her every word
for Cheetos. Her ankles bathed
in ocean waves
halleluiah-hand raised,
she calls her children
all by the same name.

# If Only

*Shuttle-cock and battle-door*
*A little pink-love*
*And feathers are strewn.*
      Mina Loy

Hidden in the toolshed, we
took turns

backing each other
against the wall

next to the rake and spade
and dust-coated cobwebs

laced to the teeth
of a rusty saw

hung by the windowsill, where
the husk of a moth's better self

lay discarded at the altar
of a wolf spider's funnel.

If only we had quit that
sweltering summer in the shed—

if only we'd been more aware
that gas fumes leaked

from the mower cooped inside
would mingle

with the smell of raunchy
grass-mulch caked to the blades.

## Call Before You Dig

This is a cautionary tale—
of cryptic glyphs in day-glow orange
scrawled across my lawn, blue
along the sidewalk, a story of hidden

gas lines, cables, all things buried,
of how I've spent my life afraid
to dig, denying a taste for dirt,
a lust to root in rich black clay,

to feel it ooze between my toes
yet all the while wallow-phobic
praying to remain unsoiled.
No wonder when the snow fell

I became self-interred
confined to solitary, listening
to inside voices beneath the covers
of my favorite goose-down comforter

with all the other smothered bodies.
Found dug up: wrist bone relic
of a Bodhisattva wearing Jimmy Hoffa's
handcuffs. Call before you dig.

# Earthshine

I can see both
the fingernail moon
and its shadow glow,

the *albedo*
of what isn't—
just not both at once

like face and vase,
duck and rabbit
through the windshield
wiper squeaking.

Dusk, the equinox light
stretches the estuary wider
than my peripheral
wisdom. A flock
of thrift-store salt and pepper shakers
lifts off honking *O' Canada*.

March blizzard, Spring
a maybe, yet
I'm finally certain
I love someone

else. No more
snow-day rye in my coffee,
no more myth of a fork in the road.
I can't take myself back. There's nothing
good about me except

*everyday above ground*
my accountant friend tells me
*is a good day* no matter
what the clichés are saying.

Morning arrives, the vernal chorus
from the marsh
sings praise-songs to the sun.

## Awe is Real
*I respond silently mouth open wide*
*as a bowl of curd freshly solidified.*
        Durga Lal Shrestha


### I. McGuffey's Reader
*The man. A pen.*
*The man has a pen.*

Awe overwhelms me
suddenly gape-mouthed,

knee deep in weeds,
my heart
arrhythmic with the secret

code of winter
rain, dots and dashes
on my yellow slicker
                    means something

different to each,
so I pull back my hood,

look around, have the foggiest
ideas, surrounded
by nuclear-age concrete bunkers,
cracks alive
with florescent green moss.

Glancing down—
            my galoshes
are still unbuckled. Now, let's check

your reading comprehension:

What's a slicker?
What's a galosh?

## II: Corn Dogs
*...impaled on sticks and dipped in batter.*
        Abstract of Patent

From the privileged view
of the shampooed

county-fair, blue-ribbon
goat, nose poking through the slats

the two of us smell

like sex—
        each holding our pink

hornet's nest
of cotton candy

as we tease off synonyms

for fear, reverence, wonder, desire
all swirled into
                awe

the kind philosophers call
'The Sublime'

to wafer on each other's tongue.

### III. Voting Rights Act
*At what time of day on January 20 each four years*
*does the term of the president of the United States end?*
         Alabama Voter "Literacy" Test

Awe with neither
beauty nor truth

is terror. Suddenly
I remember

why I'm in line
following arrows

chalked on cement,
what's left
of the esplanade, cracked

pavement overgrown
with milkweed thistle,
cotton loose in the wind.

I roll back my eyes,
try to recall

companionship
and broken
bread. The morning

after—
         awful dread

tossed on my doorstep—
                         hand-torn clouds,
ragged skies,
another squall of news.

## IV. Oldies Station

*We be three poor mariners*
*Newly come from the seas;*
*We spend our lives in jeopardy*
*While others live at ease.*
          English ballad

Awe will appear
as unintended
agency—
say, the ocean

between my ears,
a playlist
algorithm

random as sand fleas
dancing
on crab shells
gleaned by gulls.

Meanwhile gale force winds

flatten the dune grass
sending skittish birds
to shelter

in coastal groves
of gnarled Sitka spruce bent

in awe
of the off-shore Will.

Listen—
        another white-crowned sparrow

rewinds
that same old cassette.

# Four

## Elegy for an Election

We've nothing left but the rind of ourselves
    peeled from the whole,
        pared like an orange

globe, a Mercator projection, our future
    pinned to the classroom wall
        by alien cartographers. Two months ago,

when the polar axis wobbled
    away from true north, when the sky ignited
        screen-saver colors, when the otherworldly

spacecraft landed, as I was raising her cusp to my lips
    her back arching, gasping,
        pulling my hair. And then we watched TV

like the rest—us and the billions. Earth, the networks
    called it early, now a mere crossroad midden
        where they've come

to bury their afterbirth, dump their trash
    and advertise the rapture. How to commemorate
        our own apocalypse, how to observe? We sit

in orange Naugahyde chairs, playing gin rummy
    in a double-wide. I'm so happy I chain smoke Kools,
        sip Seven and Seven. Our eyes gaze up

tracking the ceiling fan strobe illusion,
    shadows paddling backward. Even the cat's confused,
        swatting at empty air.

## Learning Curve

When I found out screech owls don't—actually
they whistle and trill
desire and defense—I cringed. Turns out
it was a barn owl screeching
from its hole in a sycamore all night
that reminded me of hearing

my girlfriend's pleasure through the wall
next door while I munched cold pizza
with my dealer, Rachel, from across the hall
and tried not to stare
at her shriveled arm, or mispronounce *thalidomide*
asking nonchalant. I didn't expect she'd let me in

or call me out on just how cruelly
everyone gawked when she dropped
her cafeteria tray, tater-tots rolling
across the tiles, or how cruel
we all have been to let that *fucker Johnson*
call up more troops

for his dirty war—even crueler
the cute lifeguard never returned
home to our city pool. *He was always
kind to me*, she said, *it's always
kids like him*—whose dad worked the line
at Ford River Rouge, stood with the union,

got beat up by company thugs. Dense
as I am, I was unaware it was so
late when she leaned her cheek
on my shoulder, exhaled a smoky
*fuckin'-A*, and passed me back the bong
asking, do you—did you—know him?

## See and Be Seen

Dawn, as advertised, a mirror
lake reflecting a mountain
swept with white mare's tails,

two no-nonsense Quinault women
in park-ranger khaki rearrange deck chairs
on the patio outside the lodge

overlooking the lawn sloped gently
down to the lake, a dock,
a row of canoes beached

on a small strip of sand.
In the lodge, breakfast,
*Please Wait To Be Seated*,

a party of three—red-haired boy,
bathed and combed, leans sleepily
against his mother. The dad insists

on a table next to the window
with one-way glass
for them to watch the hummingbirds

up close as they lunge, parry,
hover and bluff, each
battling for a place at the feeder.

## Restless Leg Syndrome

Aroused from scofflaw sleep
with traces of blue
and pink salt
on my tongue, from the window

I watch the moon bathe
a slash-heap of broken family
trees from last spring's
*ice storm of the century*, bulldozed
into a burn pile waiting.

The true purpose of morning
lost, I learn, in an Oregon rain
forest thick with remorse,
I'm not the only one complicit,

the sun dealing chlorophyll
to the oak and maple, gentrified
old growth tracts where ferns
once slept with rotting fir logs,
moss-shagged, lusty as rust.

Which is to say, it takes a lot
to wake up, let alone love
bacon sputtering in the skillet
since words don't work anymore

tromping through cold
oatmeal congealed in a pot on the stove
searching for buried raisins, commuting
through wrist-cutting blackberry
bramble traffic entwining the mirrored city.

Still, I have no doubt
*today's the day* all over again,
ceiling fan reasoning
circularly—*same old, same old, same old* eyes

once more window shopping
for second-hand jam jars,
tongue too short to lick the bottom,
silver spoons locked away in the hutch.

## Ode to the Fern

Tabernacled in the forest,
cloistered in fern, two wrens
lob ontological proofs
across the no-man's land.

I listen entranced
to light-hearted drizzle
in half-light dancing
patty-cake with broad-leaf maples.
The pond reflects on the moment

a heron achieves an epiphany
spearing a frog. But soon enough
the wind
riles the perfect surface
rekindling old addictions
to mirrors. My path

continues to serpentine
among the old-growth
trunks, ribbon-tied
with empirical questions,
tagged graffiti orange
like boxcars. A voice

warns do not speak
the Latin name
of the red columbine,
The Deceiver, who claims
*I'm a Tang dynasty lantern*
*Look at me dangle!*

Instead, praise the mystery—
whose fingers first
brushed the spores underside the fronds
releasing the private language of ferns.

## Ins and Outs
*Draw a circle—whatever's inside it is the poem.*
*Everything else is the world.*
          Campbell McGrath


Nesting in the eaves of the 1890s hotel, now
a retreat and mindfulness center,
purple finches garble the message. Turns out,
Finch-speak lacks the antonym pair, *inside/outside*.
Birdbrains can't comprehend Venn diagrams.

In the garden out back, we wonder aloud
are the koi in the Zen pond mouthing
the scared syllable *OM*
or just vacuuming algae-coated stones?

Water-striders skate the pond's surface
like Christmas in Rockefeller Square.
But Siri says eastern Oregon.
We believe her. There's a California quail

on a fencepost tossing back his curl
like a teenage heartthrob. A kestrel
with a mouse in its talons plays Cirque du Soleil
on a telephone wire. Two mourning doves
watch a pickup late for church
racing down a gravel road,
but none of us know anything
about the message.

Outside the fence, a field of green hay,
freshly mown, layered in rows,
the sky above patrolled by balding vultures
searching for diced up snakes and voles,
the local farmhouse mouser claiming
it hunts only because of instinct, and takes
no pleasure in the kill.

The finches are duly skeptical
and chorus *with a varied warble*
*that begins with slightly blurry notes.*

The hotel is surrounded by black-locust trees,
tops eye-level with our second floor window.
Dried seed pods hang shriveled
into spiral wind-toys,
rattling like teeth in the breeze
or fallen scattered across the lawn.
Urban-landscaper types from Portland
call it a *nuisance tree*. I fear that I understand.

Beyond this oasis, up the highway,
two ghost towns and halfway in-between,
a lone roadside rock-shop,
shelves overloaded with thunder eggs,
halved and polished,
it's run by a sun-leathered trans
in a beaded headband
*from Orange Country, originally,*
we learn without having to ask.

The rest is grass
and cattle—Trump country.

Towards dusk, a flock of goldfinch
undulates across the road
to land whistling in a ditch
of Queen Anne's Lace and dry thistle.

From a cottonwood
straddling the boundary-line creek,
a Bullock's oriole trills
sharp and clear his territorial aria.
Soon, when the snow on the peaks
is gone forever, this jubilant creek

will turn to dust. Or so the finches
seem to blurb and garble—
too many *B*s and *R*s and *L*s
to really make sense
of what they're trying to say.

## Boon

Halfway between Burns and Vale, the highway
follows the Malheur River double-yellow
hairpin turns through the canyon. In June,
for twenty odd years, driving back and forth
from the fiddle festival at Weiser, we'd pass
the same faded plastic flowers stapled
to crosses. Our favorite spot to rest by the water

was a narrow pull-out under a cottonwood,
leafy thick, full of footwear and wonder—
who first took their old pair of sneakers,
tied them together, tossed them high on a limb
to snag—no one knows why—some folks
said gang-sign—but we too once lobbed our own
torn K-Mart knock-offs and later a single

flip-flop. One year, we spied a shiny pair
of Nikes sacrificed on high. Over time,
it seemed more pilgrim caravans must
have stood beneath the tree, like us, to test
their arms and true aims, to adorn it
with laced-up fruit, hung in season and decay.
When the tree stopped leafing, it remained

an altar to absurdity, a shrine
to the mundane pace of everyday waste—but maybe
I'm reading too much meaning into it. Mostly
people just pulled over because it was
one of the few places along the way
for folks like us to get a break, perhaps
change a baby's diaper, wipe up vomit

from a car-sick toddler, take a leak, or grab
a sandwich from the cooler to eat beneath
the tree we all could see was dying. I heard
it got blown down and washed away in a storm.
All the same, to have rested even once
in its pedestrian shade, if not exactly
a blessing was, at the very least, a boon.

## Continental Divide

*...our body is a moulded river.*
    Novalis

*Education is not preparation for life;*
*education is life itself.*
    John Dewey


Months of rain, the soil's had it up to here, spontaneous overflow

recollected in depressions across the road. A poet I know

says this scans poorly—*crazy weather we've been having.* Most folks
                                                                    just take video

of the flooded Riverfront Park underwater. Celebrity osprey

perched on the swing set, the children's slide mostly submerged

trailing a wake like a German U-boat through caramel current. A knock-
                                                                     kneed shorebird

on its Arctic journey wades the curbside waterline, where until yesterday

the *Hot Tamales* food-truck parked—*A rising tide lifts all boats*—
                                                                        is the expression

made famous, I believe, by Reagan,

but known for centuries by the Chinese,

who are still being blamed for the virus clinging to the nose-wiped sleeves

of two home-schoolers raised in a bus, by their anti-vaxxer mom who
                                                                           yet believes

in driving them to the library each week for stories and poems. Come June

they'll drive to Idaho's fiddle festival, then on to Missouri to learn a tune

from a good ol' boy, turned ninety-six. T*welve years old,*

*when I learned to play*, he says, *from this nice colored fella, been a slave.*

Then on to Clifftop and afterwards, Galax. The course of life,
                the kids are told:

to camp for free in national forests, sing harmony on murder ballads,
                  and nightly rave

with the old-timey folk on banjo and fiddle—*New River, Duck River,*

*Big Sandy, Salt River*, to embody the course of water.

## Step in the Same River Twice

Heraclitus says we can't, but then again, he's never been to Utah.
He would never understand how two geeks could meet through math
inside the curly brackets, both wanting to follow the order of operations,
and how at dinner, we'd discover a scatter plot of poppy seeds

on a white tablecloth and scribble together on a Sazerac-stained napkin
the formula for *why not* leave Salt Lake, rent a Prius, drive due west,
and doing eighty-five, calculate the path of a hawk lifted off
from the ditch exploding on our grill. He couldn't predict how

a gravel truck rattles past, shooting pebbles, how our windshield
wisecracks about the sky, although he should have seen
at midnight how oncoming brights from a bully pickup rushing
drunk towards us cried *Repent! Repent!* Luckily, a jerk of the wheel

saves us onto the shoulder, where we weep, hug, kiss, fuck
under the hatchback, fall asleep. I'm certain he never dreamed
of an Oregon high desert sunrise, or watched the John Day river
snuggle a cliff, curl into a pool across from where we stand

together on a pebble shore. We sacrifice our bacon fat from the skillet
to the god of fire, say a prayer, then step goose-bump naked, clasping hands,
two souls in the same river once, as the current, so revered
by the esteemed philosopher, struggles to grasp the simple idea of feet.

# Five

## Afterimage

Queen Anne's Lace,
common name *wild
carrot*, dry and shriveled
in a roadside ditch,
scratched across my face

as if some middleman
rubbed his whiskers
against my cheek,
some exegete
with deep set eyes

and ravines of wrinkles
eroded by spring
runoff into storm drains.
Everyone already knew
the back story, the myth

of gravity and its agents
of least resistance—water,
a given, guttered through grates
down to a sunless place,
where pale fish suspend weightless,

blind in turquoise pools. Pretend
it happened only once—imagine
myself as a mirror lake, perfection
flawed by the rings of hungry trout
rising to feed on the hatch.

## Mayfly Diary
*The insect lives and flies about until the evening,*
*but as the sun goes down it pines away,*
*and dies at sunset having lived one day,*
*from which circumstance it is called the 'ephemeron'.*
         Aristotle, *History of Animals*, Book 5


Today—is my birthday, my death day, my body

grapple-hooked from the river, low

serotonin wearing the pants in the family,

kid gloves buried with the hatchet

in the backyard next to the pet lizard.

Each has its own line of accessories;

each counts as a life.

## Mayfly Diary

*There are certain Flyes, that are called Ephemera, that liue but a day.*
　　　　1626　F. Bacon *Sylua Syluarum*, OED


Today—is my birthday, my death day, dawn

sky drooping peaches, a silver bell

and a pomegranate. Early light, purple finches

perched on a grapevine wake and bake

while old crows bicker in a Douglas fir.

In the evening, a black and white calf

wearing a garland of marigold

grazes on garbage dumped at the crossroad.

## Mayfly Diary

*Mayflies spend most of their lives in the water as nymphs
and then emerge as adults...*
        National Wildlife Federation

Today—is my birthday, my death day, even

in cinnamon light refracted through a bottle of rye,

or a fly on the wall blending in with the stucco,

it's still me

peering into the hand-swiped portal

of a steamed mirror

and spotting the Book of Agog

hurtling toward me out of the fog.

## Mayfly Diary

*Mayfly adult longevity is rather short,*
*not exceeding one nuptial flight for most.*
        Annual Review of Entomology

Today—is my birthday, my death day, Sunday

morning waking up on the floor

to a choir of ladybugs

rubbing their spots with spot remover,

my eyes wander off,

follow the floorboards

to power-strip cords tangled this way

and that, all trying to mate

with any whatsit they can plug.

## Mayfly Diary

*They mate, and the males usually fall to the water*
*in a near death state with outstretched wings*
*that anglers call "spent."*
        Fly Fisherman Magazine

Today—is my birthday, my death day, I'm told

collecting June bugs, spurs caught in the screen door,

then giving each a name, will get me into the DSM-5,

but it's nothing like the sun

getting totaled by the moon then towed to a scrapyard

while we flay our skin with Naphtha soap

and toss our unclean clothes in the fire.

## Mayfly Diary

*They are a primitive order of insects, and their elegance and delicate lives have made them popular beyond the world of trout fishing.*
     Troutnut.com

Today—is my birthday, my death day, finally

it all comes down to this—no one

knits mittens in this town

full of gloves made from the skin

of someone else's god—but suppose

next winter, Snowy Owl alights on a pile of coal

while voles join threesomes to keep from freezing,

then it's more than a theory, this natural world.

## Nature/Nurture

A loaf of wild chimpanzees
plays fifty-two pickup
with a deck of DNA.
Schools of thought
swim through
the soup. Cerebellums

catch fire,
sing to the moon
until the gibbous phase
unleashes rivers of viscera
grinning from tools. Bones
of contention,

the battle of rice
versus millet, in the wink
of a scythe wheat falls
into bushels
of smallpox. Oracles
etched on tibia, spells

baked on clay tablets
mutate into scrolls
unrolled by priests
hording the script, dismaying
the pestles of working
mothers. A box of rain,

a limestone fugue,
aqueducts built for gardens
greened with rational numbers,
and thus once more—the gall of death
climbs the spiral staircase
to down another shot, and dance
the Nataraja.

# Six

## For Araniko
*To his superb skill, all lands pay tribute.*
>From an inscription, 1316, Gangziyuan, China,
>memorializing the Newāh artist and architect, Araniko,
>written by a Chinese contemporary, Cheng Jufu.

*Kathmandu, February 24, 2020*


Can a virus cross the Himalayas
like the Four Noble Truths,
or a horse-caravan carrying loads of salt?

How about silver
engraved ritual bowls and plates,
or bronze Bodhisattvas crafted

by Kathmandu artisans, patronage
for shrines and sacred
monasteries in Tibet,

hauled over the mountains, eluding
bandit, blizzard,
avalanche and altitude sickness?

Can a virus cross the Himalayas
like Araniko, carrying art, sculpture,
architecture, contagious

memes to Lhasa
and beyond
to the court of Kublai Khan?

Can a virus cross the Himalayas,
landing non-stop like a Dragon Air flight
Guangzhou to Kathmandu?

## Sense and Reference
*Patan, Nepal*

I sit at a tea stall

    *A hawk circles, hunting above the temple,*

trying to recall the name
for this round flat pastry,
but end up merely pointing—

    *pigeons clapping panicked into the sky.*
    *A chittering troop of monkeys*

*malpā,* the owner explains
it tastes very *mākhu.*

    *scrambles for cover*
    *from the passing shadow,*

I try one—*mākhu?*
*mākhu,* she repeats.

    *scurrying under roof-struts*
    *carved with erotica,*

I'm confused, same word

    *twos and threesomes*
    *wrapped in tantric embrace*

for the taste of soybean,
pudding, rice flakes, curd,
pancake, banana,
almond? Avocado too

    *to protect the wooden pagoda*
    *I'm told*

says my Newāh friend
who's been to Texas.

    *from the prudish*

Clearly, I have no taste

    *virgin goddess of lightning.*

and no clue.

## Ordinary Language

*What is the difference between searching for a word in memory
and searching for a friend in the park?*
       Wittgenstein

Let us attack the question
first by asking the slide rule
how a worker feels
getting laid off

then ask the red-nectar feeder
what it thinks about
hummingbirds choosing
smack over fuchsia.

Now translate this into emoji,
just to see how meaning gets lost,
traded-off for '68 Tigers baseball cards.
Some of us explode at the thought,

act out in daycare, throw letter blocks.
Some of us get stoned
behind the wheel until an unmarked
song comes along on the radio

pulls us over, catches us weeping—we fess up
sputtering like summer sprinklers,
trying to endure the starling's jeer
from a dead oak, trusting the night

shift to clean up the mess. *It's so easy
to misconstrue* is no excuse—in any case,
*Hey, you're quite the grilled-cheese sandwich*
was never a compliment, more

like a threat—even Humpty Dumpty
knows he's liable
to take home the wrong
pair of pants from the cleaner.

## GṚDHRAKŪṬA

I'll translate for you—
'Vulture Peak,'
or better yet, 'Buzzard Butte,'

where the Buddha turned
the Second Wheel of Law:
*Self is illusion.*

Damn confusing!
Try to picture yourself
as a hollow gourd

carved with a Jack-O-Lantern's grimace,
seeds scooped out, salted, baked
into a snack,

the rest pulped into pie.
Picture light through the holes
you call eyes.

Picture your candle melted
flat, soon a frozen puddle
of wax.

Picture fuzzy, blue-gray mold,
the rot
as your bankrupt shell

corporation collapses.
And yet, your monkey brain
chitters on

all through lunch
with your reptile brain
and voluptuous Tara,

who points to the rusty
lettuce on your plate
declaring—*that salad is sad.*

## Recursion

Once again, time for the gulls'
morning commute to the landfill,

time for the minus tide,
time for winter to be unraveled,

ocean baffled in fog. A cobalt bowl
on her bungalow steps

with agate and sage steeped in brine
all night beneath the new

moon, she cups it,
raises it to her forehead,

then presses it to her lips, mouthing
an unheard-of prayer.

Across the street, an osprey
high in a Sitka spruce

whistles and chirps
the pros and cons of death

and afterwards earthly
rebirth. Beneath the tree

a newly painted yellow curb
begins to glow, sunrise

golden lit as if
an illumined manuscript.

*Dissociation disorder?* she asks.
*Yep,* I reply—*always been this way.*

## Language Lesson

Due north of sweet
mango summer's slippery pulp
between the teeth

or frothy *chia*
in fog-bound winter, steaming
cardamom and clove—

far east of bitter greens, garlic
and a pouty little fruit, *amli*
in hot and sour soup—

west of the fire, flesh from the butcher,
fresh green chili fried,
with fingerfulls of pounded rice flakes

and grandma's moonshine, *ayela*, poured
high from a narrow spout, bubble
eyes splashing in a shallow clay cup—

south of the salt
trade, Buddha's footfalls,
ancient paths along the paddy,

where anklets jangle gracefully past
tender shoots impatient
for the monsoon to mount the Himalayas—

there's a place on the tongue,
chew slowly, savor…
a moment English cannot reach.

# Notes

**I entreat myself.** Selections of Durga Lal Shrestha's poetry come from my translation of his Nepal Bhasa (Newari) poem collection, *The Blossoms of Sixty-Four Sunsets*. Durga Lal Shrestha (b. 1936) is Nepal's best-known living poet.

The Newāh (Newar) themselves are the ancestral people of the Kathmandu valley, responsible for its cultural heritage of literature, art, and architecture, but they are now a minority in the country of Nepal as a whole. Their language, Nepal Bhasa, is part of the Trans-Himalayan (Tibeto-Burman) language family. Although it has been strongly influenced by contact with Indic languages, such as Sanskrit, the language's Himalayan and highland Southeast Asian historical roots distinguish it from the Indic languages, including Nepali, the national *lingua franca*. Following the Nepali-speaking Gurkha dynasty's conquest of the Kathmandu valley in 1768, and the establishment of the Shah, and later Rana, regimes, Newāh language and culture has been continuously subjected to systematic discrimination, and sometimes brutal suppression, including the destruction of books and the imprisonment of writers. It is now considered an endangered language.

The word translated as 'entreat' in the title of the poem is *jvajalapā*, which, although similar to the familiar 'namaste' used throughout Nepal, is used only between Nepal Bhasa speakers. It may, in many cases, be understood as a greeting, but it can also mean 'honor,' 'salute,' 'bid,' (cf. I *bid you good day*) or 'request, entreat' (cf. *Would you do me the honor of...*). It is the latter sense that is appropriate in this poem. A translation such as 'I honor myself,' interestingly similar to Whitman's 'I celebrate myself,' would be a whimsical, but inaccurate translation.

**Saṃsāra** (page 10). The elephant-boy refers to the Hindu deity Ganesh, highly revered throughout South Asia. In the story of Ganesh's childhood, his father, Lord Siva, comes home and mistaking him for an insolent rival, cuts off his head. At the insistence of Ganesh's mother, Parvati, Siva is granted the ability to bring his son back, but with a proviso—Siva can only restore him based on the first animal he sees, which turns out to be an elephant. In Buddhism, the term *saṃsāra* refers to the cycle of mundane struggle and pain, through endless birth, death, and rebirth, the release from which is obtained through the teachings of the Buddha.

**News at Eleven** (page 13). For those of you keeping score at home, the poem is hendecasyllabic.

**Estimated Time of Arrival** (page 14). Kathmandu's Tribhuvan International Airport is rated one of the least safe airports in the world. The epigraph, *C'est le Christ qui monte au ciel mieux que les aviateurs / Il détient le record du monde pour la hauteur*, comes from Guillaume Apollinaire's *Zone*, translated by William Meredith.

**River** (page 15). This is my own translation of the poem 'River' by Cittadhar Hṛdaya, the most important Newāh poet in the 20th century revival of Nepal Bhasa poetry. During the brutal period of Rana rule (1847-1950), writing in the Nepal Bhasa language was considered subversive and during the 1930s, Cittadhar himself spent five years in jail for writing poetry. The poem 'River' likely reflects Chittadhar's experience traveling to Calcutta, where his poems, prohibited from being published in Kathmandu, could find publishers.

**Lunch with Gautam** (page 19). Hungry Ghosts: "...beings that have very, very tiny mouths...and great stomachs; and these stomachs are empty..." from Tibetan Buddhist Altar (Jetsunna Ahkon Lhamo).

**God of the Gaps** (page 27). Arjun is the hero of the *Bagavad Gita*, a verse segment embedded in the Sanskrit epic *The Mahabharata*. Facing a momentous battle against some of his own kin, with carnage and bloodshed certain on all sides, Arjun seeks moral counsel from his charioteer, the god Krishna. The ensuing verse-dialog covers the most fundamental tenets of Hindu belief, in particular, the notion of *dharma*, variously understood as duty, moral obligation, right, law. In other representations, Krishna is depicted with blue skin, an alluring, non-binary, amorous cowherd, playing the flute.

**Prān** (page 28). Godavari refers here to the botanical gardens and adjacent temple located on the southern edge of the Kathmandu valley.

**Continental Divide** (page 58). In the epigraph to "River Profile," Auden translates Novalis '...*unser Körper ein gebildeter Fluss ist...*' as 'our body is a moulded river' using English 'moulded' for German '*gebildeter*.' The root itself, 'form, image, shape, picture,' also appears in *bildung*, as in *Bildungsroman*, i.e., novels depicting the education and character formation of a hero. The exact meaning and English translation of the term *Bildung* has its own cottage industry of scholarly debate, variously 'formation,' 'education,' 'enculturation.'

**Mayfly Diary I** (page 64). 'ephemera' from Greek, *epi* 'for,' *hemera* 'a day.'

**For Araniko** (page 73). The 12th century Newāh artist, Araniko, traveling to Tibet and later China, was renowned for bringing firsthand knowledge of the innovative styles of Newāh art and architecture, with its early Mahayana Buddhist influences, from the Kathmandu Valley to Lhasa, and later to the court of Kublai Khan's Yuan Dynasty in China, where he resided and ultimately passed away in 1306. His reputation in Kublai Khan's court, as an artist, architect, and craftsman is recorded by a Chinese contemporary, the writer Cheng Jufu. Available histories suggest that Araniko was born into a family of Sakya Newāh in the Kathmandu Valley, who specialized in silver/bronze craftwork and sculpture. The Tuladhar Newāh were responsible for much of the important trans-Himalayan trade network between Kathmandu and Lhasa, which lasted up until the Chinese occupation of Tibet.

**Ordinary Language** (page 75). Humpty Dumpty, from Lewis Carroll, *Through the Looking Glass*: "When I use a word," Humpty Dumpty said, in rather a scornful tone, "it means just what I choose it to mean—neither more nor less." "The question is," said Alice, "whether you can make words mean so many different things."

**Gṛdhrakūṭa** (page 76). Gṛdhrakūṭa is a sacred spot in the state of Bihar, northern India, the location where the historical Buddha gathered his community of devotees to deliver what has now become the most important teachings in the Buddhist canon.

# Acknowledgments

Thanks to the following publications where poems from this manuscript, sometimes in different versions or titles, appear.

| | |
|---|---|
| *Maintenant* | Vacancies |
| *Comstock Review* | Rule of Threes |
| *Hiram Poetry Review* | Umbra |
| *North Dakota Quarterly* | Ordinary Language |
| *Naugatuck River Review* | Learning Curve |
| *Passages North* | Biopsy |
| *Pacifica Literary Review* | What I Wanted |
| *Modern Poetry Quarterly Review* | Prosthetic |
| *Magnolia Review* | Prāṇ |
| *PacificREVIEW* | Step in the River Twice |
| *Sow's Ear Poetry Review* | Recognition, The Library Window |
| *The Black Boot* | If Only |
| *Bending Genres* | Ins and Outs, Earthshine |
| *Poets/Artists* | Nature/Nurture |
| *POEM* | Language Lesson |
| *Hubbub* | Backwards Through the Dark |

My deepest thanks to the many poets over the years who have supported me with valuable criticism and encouragement in equal measures: John Morrison, Rachel Barton, Michael Malan, Thom Ward, Roger Weingarten, Charlotte Pence, and the late Peter Sears. I also want to thank Larry Moore and Broadstone Books for having faith in my work and supporting this project through to completion. Thanks also to Western Oregon University for the support provided via a Faculty Development Grant. I'm especially grateful to Natalie E. Laswell for giving me permission to use her painting "Running Out of Words" for the cover of this book.

I would not have been able to continue throughout the years of writing and rewriting, with seemingly little to show for my efforts, were it not for the countless hours of fishing, drinking and discussing poetry with my good friend, poet Henry Hughes. Henry, this book would not exist without you!

Lastly, the very idea of me writing a book of my own poems would never have occurred to me were it not for the profound inspiration and honor in getting to know Nepal Bhasa poet Durga Lal Shrestha through translating his poetry, and especially in conversations with him. My attempts to comprehend and translate his unique poetic sensibilities would not have been possible without the insights of my friends and partners during the long process (R. Manandhar, Daya Shakya, and my dearly missed friend, Rajendra Shrestha) to whom I give again my heartfelt thanks.

## About the Author

Born in Detroit, living in Oregon, David Hargreaves' translated collection *The Blossoms of Sixty-Four Sunsets* by Nepal Bhasa (Newāh) poet Durga Lal Shrestha was published in 2014, Kathmandu, Nepal, in a dual-language format. He is a professor of Linguistics at Western Oregon University.